A selection of comments
at the first professional read

"*Le Bourgeois gentilhomme* is a very d
This adaptation has a through line,
the characters are much easier to fo...

"In this play we can recognise the characters that existed, and these immediately resonate with some of the people we meet nowadays."

"It's very appropriate in the social circumstances we live in today."

"The writing was absolutely brilliant. It was sparkling, witty, so clever, so much information in each line, *and* it was in verse."

"The language was extremely accessible for the modern audience, although also in keeping with the period."

"What I particularly liked about it was the dexterity of the verse. It didn't sound like a translation. It sounded as if it had been written by a British poet."

"I was utterly gripped. I really wanted to know what happened next."

"It was absolutely bursting with rhymes. This drove the action forward."

"It had enormous energy. I laughed the whole way through."

"It held my attention for every moment, and I loved it."

"I think it's going to appeal to lots and lots of people, and I think it'll go down very well indeed. It's dynamic. It's original. People can relate to it. The characters are all very different. I think you've got something very special here."

* *The rehearsed reading by Actors & Writers London, on 24th January 2011, was directed by Kenneth Michaels, and performed by Peter Saracen, Rosalind Adler, Nadia Ostacchini, Edmund Dehn, Denys Graham, Richard Ward, Simon Brandon, Lee Peck, Kirsty Bennett, Ingrid Evans, Jeryl Burgess and Rosemary Francis, with music by Will Gormley and Paddy Gormley.*

About Paddy Gormley, who translated and adapted the play

Paddy Gormley finds great beauty in the rhythms and assonances of spoken English. He also takes delight in challenging conventional wisdom, finding that scepticism and doubt, far from being negative forces, are pathways to new ideas. These factors have led him to develop proseverse, a style of writing that flows as effortlessly and meaningfully as prose, but uses the rhythmic patterns and (often internal) rhymes associated with verse. Paddy Gormley's proseverse plays include not only *The Social Climber*, but also his first Molière adaptation, *Misanthrope II* (1995), and his modern verse drama *Twenty-Twenty* (2001).

Paddy Gormley's interests in language, creativity and metaphysics are reflected in, and informed by, the wider body of his work as analytical writer, presenter, teacher and facilitator.

www.excitingwriting.info

About Michael Baldwin, who provided the illustrations

Michael Baldwin has been designing costumes since the late 1950s. His West End shows include *Chrysanthemum* and two Molière productions at the Old Vic. He was a costume designer for Associated Rediffusion TV and London Weekend Television for ten years, and was nominated for the BAFTA Costume Design Award for *Worzel Gummidge*.

Michael Baldwin has designed the costumes for ten films including *Madame Sin* (Bette Davis, Robert Wagner), *Theatre of Blood* (Vincent Price, Diana Rigg), *Quatermass* (Sir John Mills, Simon McCorkindale), *The Great McGonagal* (Spike Milligan, Peter Sellers) and *The Rolling Stones Rock and Roll Circus* (Mick Jagger, John Lennon).

His 300 Pop video credits include costumes for Freddie Mercury, Bonnie Tyler, Ultravox and Duran Duran.

www.michaelbaldwin.org.uk

The Social Climber

Molière's
Le Bourgeois gentilhomme

translated and adapted
by
Paddy Gormley

illustrated
by
Michael Baldwin

LogoS

First published by Logos Theatre Company, August 2011
www.logostheatre.co.uk

Printed by MPG Books
www.mpg-booksgroup.com

FSC
Mixed Sources
Product group from well-managed forests and other controlled sources
www.fsc.org Cert no. TT-COC-1977
© 1996 Forest Stewardship Council

A CIP record for this book is available from the British Library.

ISBN 978-0-9569678-0-0

Contents

Foreword by Paddy Gormley

Le Bourgeois gentilhomme is late Molière, written in 1670, just three years before his death, and after more than a decade working under the patronage of Louis XIV. It is perhaps one of the best known Molière play-titles, all of which date from that same period of fifteen years. And yet it is far from the best known of Molière's works.

It does not deserve to be so neglected. *Le Bourgeois gentilhomme* is, after all, the only Molière play to address the evergreen issue of social climbing. Accordingly, it cannot be excluded from the canon of Molière's satires on human foibles–misanthropy, hypocrisy, miserliness, hypochondria, and so on. But this is not its sole recommendation.

The relative neglect of *Le Bourgeois gentilhomme* probably stems from the fact that is not just a play, but a comédie-ballet–a music theatre spectacular for the court of Louis XIV. The king's patronage also embraced the Italian born composer Jean-Baptiste Lully, and *Le Bourgeois gentilhomme* is probably the most famous collaboration between Molière and Lully.

But the extent of this collaboration presents a daunting challenge for 21st century theatre producers. In addition to the large cast of actors that is a familiar feature of 17th century plays, *Le Bourgeois gentilhomme* also calls for extravagant musical resources, including a grand assemblage of instruments.

No less importantly, the structure of the piece is out of step with the expectations of modern theatre audiences. The first act is a musical entertainment, led by Jourdain's (the social climber's) music and dancing masters. The second act features Jourdain's dancing, fencing and philosophy lessons. The plot does not begin to unfold until the third act. Or should I say plots? The two main story-lines, whilst they both stem from Jourdain's gullibility, are not strictly interconnected.

The lesser of these concerns his deception by Dorante, a count, who funds his extravagant courtship of the marquise Dorimène by borrowing money from Jourdain. Dorante persuades Jourdain that he is merely acting as a go-between, trying to arouse the marquise's interest in Jourdain: a liaison with Dorimène might be just the thing to elevate Jourdain to the courtly circles to which he aspires. The pay-off scene, in which Jourdain hosts a dinner for Dorimène that ends disastrously, is wickedly funny and not to be missed.

The main story, insofar as it takes up more than twice the playing time of the Dorimène plot, is concerned with the marriage of Jourdain's daughter Lucile. Jourdain refuses the suit of Cléonte, dismissing him as insufficiently high born. Cleonte's valet Covielle plays up to Jourdain's social aspirations by telling him that Lucile is to marry the Grand Turk's son—Cléonte in disguise—and that Jourdain is to be elevated to the right royal rank of Mamamouchi. Again it's great fun, and of no small relevance in the present age, when appearances often seem to bear greater weight than substance.

Jourdain's down-to-earth wife and cheeky servant Nicole play their parts in both these plots, trying to make the social climber see the stupidity of his actions, undermining his relationship with Dorante and, finally, exploiting his gullibility by throwing their weight behind the Grand Turk deception.

The action between Jourdain and his wife includes a pleasing illustration of Molière's willingness to make fun of himself. Madame Jourdain reminds her social climbing husband that his father was a tradesman—a seller of cloth. It is surely no coincidence that Molière's own father, Jean Poquelin, was an upholsterer, who bought his way into the royal court.

In adapting *Le Bourgeois gentilhomme*, I have concentrated on telling the story within the two-act structure that is more familiar to present-day audiences, ensuring that the audience goes out to the interval wanting more, and returns to be immediately caught up in a new plot development. There is still plenty of scope for music, but music no longer dominates the action.

The first act exposes Jourdain's fixation with social climbing, introduces Mme Jourdain and the servant Nicole, and sets up the two main plots. The second act brings everything to a conclusion.

The revised structure also spreads the plot lines more evenly within the play. Whereas the marriage-and-Grand-Turk plot dominates the second half of Molière's play, it begins much sooner in *The Social Climber*. This strikes me as more satisfactory from a dramatic point of view, since it gives a better suggestion of the passing of time between Cléonte's rejection, the hatching of the Grand Turk plot, and the investiture and nuptials.

The action is punctuated by three scenes based on acts 1 & 2 of *Le Bourgeois gentilhomme*, detailing Jourdain's interactions with his tutors. Whilst these scenes might seem peripheral, being unconnected with the story of the play, it occurs to me that they are important elements in the story of Molière. Jourdain demonstrates his ineptitude at music, dancing, fencing and philosophy. It is as if Molière were toadying up to his royal patron by suggesting that the lower orders are unworthy of such pursuits as fit a king. Molière certainly had good reason to be thankful for Louis XIV, whose loyal patronage continued despite the fact that Molière's exposure of others' duplicity and self-deceit had made him many enemies.

I also like to think that, in the first act of *Le Bourgeois gentilhomme*, Molière was poking fun at his collaborator, Jean-Baptiste Lully, by suggesting that Jourdain's music master was in it for the money. The resemblance between Lully and the Music Master, as imagined by costume designer Michael Baldwin (p. 29), is entirely intentional.

Finally, a few words about the verse. *Le Bourgeois gentilhomme* is largely written in prose, with only the musical numbers in verse. My translation is entirely in rhyming verse, and almost all in lines of just two and three feet. I find that rhyming lines of dimeter and trimeter keep things moving along briskly. The shortness of the lines also means that phrases are often enjambed over two or three lines. Accordingly, my translation concentrates on the sense of the piece, while the rhymes are of relatively minor importance. For this reason, I invariably encourage actors to deliver my text as if it were prose, so that the audience is not distracted by the constant workings of rhythms and rhymes.

The re-structuring of Molière's play

The scenes of Molière's *Le Bourgeois gentilhomme* are re-ordered in *The Social Climber* as follows, with the aim of making the play more accessible to 21st century audiences.

• Jourdain's tailor brings his new suit, inviting the ridicule of Nicole and Mme Jourdain.	Acte II, scène v III, i-iii
• Encouraged by Mme Jourdain, Cléonte asks for Lucile's hand, but is rejected by Jourdain.	III, viii - xiii
• The music and dancing masters entertain Jourdain.	I, i & ii II, i
• Jourdain lends money to Dorante, despite Mme Jourdain's protestations. He and Dorante make arrangements for a dinner date with Dorimène.	III, iv - vii
INTERVAL	
• Covielle informs Jourdain that he is to be invested with the royal title of Mamamouchi, and that Lucile is to marry the Grand Turk's son.	V, iii & iv
• Jourdain's fencing lesson leads to a fist-fight with Jourdain's other three tutors.	II, ii & iii
• Jourdain's and Dorante's dinner for Dorimène is interrupted by the unexpected appearance of Mme Jourdain.	III, xv & xvi IV, i & ii
• Jourdain receives his first philosophy lesson.	II, iv
• Jourdain's investiture by Cléonte, disguised as the Grand Turk, is followed by the nuptials.	V, i - vi

Notes on performance, memorising and pronunciation

Whilst *The Social Climber* is written almost entirely in rhyming verse, the audience's enjoyment of the play will be greatly diminished if the rhythms and rhymes are allowed to impede the flow of ideas.

In contrast to classical pentameter, for example, in which the end of a line usually coincides with the end of a phrase, the ends of lines in *The Social Climber* merely indicate to the reader (as opposed to the listener) that a rhyme sound has just occurred, while the sense of the text often dictates that the phrase continues unbroken on the next line. Accordingly, for the most part, the text of the play is best delivered as if were prose, observing punctuation marks at all times, and pausing at the ends of lines only when there is a compelling reason to do so.

Having said all that, the fact of the short rhyming lines offers an invaluable *aide memoire* for actors seeking to commit the play to memory. Rhyming assonances are precisely patterned throughout the script, such that every fourth, sixth or ninth syllable marks a rhyme. The rhyming syllables (if not the final syllable of a line, then somewhere within the last word of the line) may be easily identified and marked as pivot points when learning the text.

When the text is delivered accurately, the rhymes will resonate naturally, unobtrusively and regularly within the actor's pattern of speech. If any rhyme sound is missing, however, or if the pattern is otherwise broken, the actor should take this as a prompt to revisit the script, in order to discover what has gone wrong.

This process of mapping pivotal rhyme sounds is particularly important for actors who are inclined to paraphrase. Insofar as paraphrasing disrupts the subliminal but discernible system of rhythms and rhymes, it may be seriously detrimental to the audience's enjoyment of the play.

The first and last syllables of the word MAMAMOUCHI are to be stressed. The second and third syllables are unstressed. The final syllable is pronounced with a soft sibilant, as in SHEEP. The correct pronunciation is best illustrated with reference to the speech in which the dancing master coaches Jourdain, on p. 66.

THE SOCIAL CLIMBER

The characters of the play

MONSIEUR JOURDAIN, social climber

MADAME JOURDAIN, his wife

LUCILE, their daughter

NICOLE, servant

CLÉONTE, in love with Lucile

COVIELLE, valet to Cléonte

DORANTE, Count, in love with Dorimène

DORIMÈNE, Marquise

MUSIC MASTER

MUSIC MASTER'S PUPIL

DANCING MASTER

FENCING MASTER

PHILOSOPHY MASTER

TAILOR

LACKEYS, MUSICIANS, CORPS DE BALLET

[LIGHTS. JOURDAIN ALONE]

JOURDAIN: Where's that wretched
tailor? He
was meant to fetch
my suit to me
an hour ago.
I'm so annoyed!
The man's so slow!
He's just devoid
of savoir faire!
To him it's neither
here nor there!
He oh-so-blithely
does whatever
he sees fit,
whatever suits
him. Why, he never—
[LAUGHS] What a wit!
You're such a hoot!
Sees *fit*—that's good—
and *suits* him—
[LAUGHS, THEN ANGRY AGAIN] Damn
and blast the stupid
fool! I am
so—[ENTER TAILOR, WHO
IMMEDIATELY STARTS DRESSING
JOURDAIN IN HIS NEW SUIT]
Where have you
been, then? You've kept
me so long waiting!
Overslept
again? You're late!
In case you hadn't

noticed, it's
past ten. It's maddening
to sit so—

TAILOR: I'm sorry! I've
been up since five!
And I've had half
a dozen staff
all beavering
away to bring
your suit to—

JOURDAIN: Spare
me your excuses!
I don't care
for them. What use is
that last pair
of silken stockings?
I can't wear
them! Too small! Shocking!
Far too tight!
I've never had a
worse pair! Frightful!
Torn two ladders
in them! Wretched.

TAILOR: They will stretch.
Just give them time.

JOURDAIN: You mean that I'm
supposed to let
them tear some more,
and they'll be better
than before?

TAILOR: But all the gentry
have them snug
these days. They're meant
to be tight, hug
the calves. That's fashion!

JOURDAIN: Balderdash!

TAILOR: I'll make them less
tight if I must.

JOURDAIN: That won't be necessary.
Just
let me see how
I look. [ADMIRES HIMSELF
IN A MIRROR] And now,
come with me. Follow
me about
the town. [CALLING] Nicole!
The lazy lout!
The world will see
my finery;
my retinue
of servants too.
Nicole! The idle
girl! They'll sidle
up and say
to me that they
are oh-so—

[ENTER NICOLE. TAILOR SLIPS AWAY UNNOTICED]

NICOLE: Eeek!

JOURDAIN: What's that?

NICOLE: Disaster!

JOURDAIN: It's you. Speak
to me.

NICOLE: Oh, Master,
what's become
of you? Has something
dreadful—? No!
It's fashion show
time, isn't it?
What a side-splitting
get-up! Absolutely
fabulous!

JOURDAIN: You ghastly
simpleton!
You dare to cast
nasturtiums on
my fine new suit!
I am your boss,
and—

NICOLE: What a hoot!
I'm at a loss
for words.

JOURDAIN: I am
a gentleman—

NICOLE: You're just a sham,
no better than
a common tradesman,

and to cap
it all, afraid
to—

JOURDAIN: I should slap
your face for that,
you little rat!
Go on, then, laugh!
[NICOLE LAUGHS] Oh, what's the use!
You're so obtuse!
Can't get the staff
these days!

[ENTER MADAME JOURDAIN]

MADAME JOURDAIN: Good grief!
It's past belief!
He's wearing the
upholstery.
I'll say you certainly
look different
in curtains.
Huh! As if
I'd be impressed
to have a jester
for a husband.
That cloth does
you little credit,
Sir. Please shed it.
You're already
trivial
enough without
having that shrill
creation shout

it from the rooftops.
What a goof
you are!

JOURDAIN: None but
a fool would laugh
at me.

MADAME JOURDAIN: Oh, shut
up! If you'd half
the common sense
of those expensive
tutors you
can't seem to do
without, you might
just see the light:
that people mock
you. You're a famous
laughing stock,
and that brings shame
on me. So end
this daft pretence
that you're a trendy
fashion buff
and have some sense.
You've got enough
clothes anyway—
you don't need these.
[JOURDAIN TURNS TO GO, BUT SHE
STOPS HIM] And I must say
I am disgusted
with your style
of life. It's just
too much. Those vile

types, so-called friends
of yours that spend
so much time here:
they're insincere.
They only pitch
camp here because
they know you're rich.
You'd think it was
a non-stop party
for your arty-farty
gang
of useless hangers-on.

NICOLE: I have
to say you're right,
Madame. That frightful,
rough riff-raff
come from the street
with muddy feet.
Those guttersnipes
don't think to wipe
them at the door.
They smear the floor.
No wonder poor
old Frances is
in such a tizzy,
on her knees
all day, just mopping
up and slopping
out that sleazy,
stinking rabble.

JOURDAIN: Shut it, babbling
idiot.

MADAME JOURDAIN: Oh no she's not!
Nicole has got
more sense than you
will ever have.
We could all do
with less palaver
about betterment
and finery.
Just get
to work at lining
up a suitable
young man
to wed our beautiful
girl, and
be quick about
it.

JOURDAIN: Do stop shouting
at me. I'm
just biding time.
If we sit tight,
our Mr Right
will come along
himself. You'll see.
There's nothing wrong
with waiting. We
aren't going to waste
our time with hasty
judgments when
so many eligible
men
will feel compelled
to come to me

on bended knee
to beg Lucile's
hand. Just wait! She'll
be all right. I,
meanwhile, apply
myself to betterment,
to letters,
music, etiquette.
I feed
my intellect
with all I need
to gain respect
among the high
and mighty.

MADAME JOURDAIN: Like
that loathsome shrike
that's always trying
to relieve
you of your spare
cash.

JOURDAIN: You deceive
yourself! Beware!
He's more important
than you give
him credit for.

MADAME JOURDAIN: The man's a spiv.

JOURDAIN: But he's well placed
at court—

MADAME JOURDAIN: A waste
of space, if you
ask me!

JOURDAIN: On truly
intimate
terms with the King.
That is a thing
we cannot rate
too highly. Yet
he deigns to let
himself come here
and volunteer
his friendship just
as if I must
be of his rank.
I cannot thank
him half enough
for all his kindness.

MADAME JOURDAIN: Pooh! That's stuff
and nonsense. Mind
your purse, that's all
I say. He'll crawl,
if need be, to
suck up to you
and make you lend
him all your money.

JOURDAIN: That's not funny.
He's my friend,
and it's the least
that I can do.

MADAME JOURDAIN: What? To be fleeced?
The more fool you!

JOURDAIN: I know he'll pay
me—

MADAME JOURDAIN: Hush! I heard
a knock. Away
with you, you nerd,
and put some proper
clothes on. Hop
to it! [EXIT JOURDAIN] Oh, how
did I allow
myself to make
such a mistake?
How could I be so stupid,
marrying such a dupe.
Now I'm forever stuck
with the lamest of lame ducks.

[ENTER CLÉONTE AND
COVIELLE]

MADAME JOURDAIN: Cléonte! This is a stroke
of luck. I have just spoken
to him. He's susceptible
to propositions
for Lucile. I've kept
away the competition
and the path is clear
for you, so have no fear
on that score. He'll be here
soon. I am quietly optimistic.
If you pop
the question here today
I think you'll go away
a happy man.

CLÉONTE: Madame,
you know how much I am

in love with your Lucile.
Like you, I can't help feeling
that our love will win
the day. I'm deeply in
your debt. May your espousal
of my cause arouse
a life-long bond between
us.

MADAME JOURDAIN: Here he is. He's seen
us. Get on! Break a leg!

[ENTER JOURDAIN,
DRESSED PLAINLY]

CLÉONTE: Monsieur, I've come to beg
your leave—if you'll permit
a little leave to let
me put to you a little
question—if you get
my meaning—such a question
as I think is best
put to you man to man,
a question such as cannot
easily be delegated,
you see.

JOURDAIN: Well?
What is it?

CLÉONTE: May I make
so bold, Sir, as to take
the liberty of being
so bold, Sir, as seeing
if you would permit
me—

JOURDAIN: Do get on with it!

CLÉONTE: —not to be denied
your daughter for my bride.

JOURDAIN: Am I to understand
you want my daughter's hand?

CLÉONTE: Indeed!

JOURDAIN: Why, certainly! —
if you will answer me
satisfactorily
in one thing I'm intent
on knowing: you're a gentleman,
I take it?

CLÉONTE: I—
you—If I may reply
in—Please forgive me if
I seem to find it difficult
to answer, but
it's not the most clear-cut
of terms. It's all too easy
for a shameless, sleazy
type to masquerade
beneath the accolade
of gentleman by virtue
of his birth. But, Sir,
the fact remains that birth's
no measure of true worth.
A gentleman, then, ought
to be one who has bought
his worth by having striven,
not one who's just given

"merit" willy-nilly.
A man's a man until
he proves himself a gentleman
in existential
terms. The posturing
of gentlemen, so-called,
is a misleading thing.
I, frankly, am appalled
that we should tolerate
it. I for one would hate
to have someone judge me
in terms of pedigree
alone. Although my parents
were good, honest, caring
folk, no doubt a prig
would think them infra dig.
Although I've had to learn
just what it takes to earn
enough to live, and tried
to plan ahead in life
so that I could provide
one day for loving wife
and family, I fear
there are those who would sneer
at me because I've had
to prove myself. I'm badly
off because I've no
inheritance. I lack
a Grandpapa's château.
I haven't got the backing
of ten generations
of fine ancestry.
My sole qualification

is that I am me.
It's folly, Sir, iniquitous!
Does it not sicken
you? Does not their blinkered
thinking make you think
that the whole system stinks?
It's a conspiracy
of mediocrity
empowered by great wealth
that holds its sway by stealth.
No man is ever treated
well till the élite
endows its worthless blessing.
Ugh, it's so depressing!

[LUCILE APPEARS, HAVING BEEN EAVESDROPPING]

LUCILE: Yes, yes! Please don't stop.
That's spoken like a proper
man! True worth is not
inheritance, but what
we make of it and of
ourselves. To be a gentleman
is to be loving,
gentle, fundamentally
good-natured. How
much better to be such
a man than one untouched
by love, in love with power
and with wealth, who knows
no proper love, but feigns
love long enough to close
the knot of marriage painlessly

round unsuspecting
spouse. What loving father
could so misdirect
a loving daughter? Rather
than great wealth and title
is a daughter's joy
the only true requital
for her love. No cloying
smiles for me from those
who smile upon a chattel.
My love's for the chosen
one, who will be at a
loss to know if all
the love he bears is love
enough. Though he be small
in wealth, he'll stand above
all else in true love's worth,
worth all the wealth on earth.

JOURDAIN: Your answer's singularly
vague, Sir. Tell me, are
you, then, or are you not
a gentleman? That's what
I want to know.

CLÉONTE: I—I—
I—No!

JOURDAIN: That settles it.
She's not for you. Goodbye!

CLÉONTE: But, Monsieur—?

MADAME JOURDAIN: Have some wit!
You and your gentlefolk!

The whole thing's past a joke.
Why must you act like we
are aristocracy?

JOURDAIN: Shut up!

MADAME JOURDAIN: Spare us your tales
about your blue blood-line.
Your father was a salesman,
just the same as mine.

JOURDAIN: Oh, there she goes again,
she and her old salesmen!
I'll grant your father may
have been, but those who say
mine was are talking through
their wotsits, just like you.
I tell you, I insist
I'll not have a plain Mister
for a son-in-law.

MADAME JOURDAIN: And I say that no awful
jumped-up bore will wed
my daughter. Better dead
than have to spend her life
entrapped as the poor wife
of some rich, overblown
balloon full of high-flown
conceit. Some simple chap
will make the girl far happier.
Some decent boy,
some honest hoi-polloi,
will make a better match.
He'll be a proper catch.

NICOLE: Quite right, Madame! Our local
squire's son makes the yokels
look intelligent.
You wonder which was meant
to be classed as a gentleman.

JOURDAIN: The cheek! How dare
you speak! We would prefer
your silence, if you please.
I have decided she's
cut out for a Marquise.

MADAME JOURDAIN:
She? A Marquise? Good God!
He can't be serious!
No! Over my dead body!
You'll bring shame on us.
No! I won't let some upper
class twit make advances
with a mind to scuppering
our daughter's chances
for the hell of it.
I never will permit
it. Think! What could be worse
than having some accursèd
son-in-law look down
his nose at us. And then
imagine, just to crown
it all, my grandchildren
ashamed to call me Grandma,
and me forced to stand
up every single time
her high and mighty, slimy
husband graces us

with his illustrious
attentions. And what if
Lucile had to be stiff
and starchy and ignore
our dear old friends next door
that we have known since she
was on her mother's knee.
Just think what they would say.
They would have a field day.
I almost see them crowding
outside, laughing loud
and long. "Oh, there's that proud
young woman with the pearls.
Why, it's old Jourdain's girl
all tarted up, hair curled.
She's gone up in the world.
Remember her granddad.
He was a canny lad.
He made his cash the hard
way: sold cloth by the yard.
I never understood
how poor folk like them could
have so much stashed away.
I can't help thinking they
were cheats. They must be paying
for it in the after-life,
for you don't have
to be too bright to twig
that no one makes the big
time being honest." That
is not the sort of chat
I want to hear. That's flat!
Go find a man that's grateful

for her, not a hateful
snob. The sort of lad
that always would be glad
to see us.

JOURDAIN: Where's your sense
of striving to improve
yourself? Why so defensive?
You're stuck in a groove
of hopeless indigence,
and I intend to move
you on. Why must you shut
yourself up in a rut
like any common slut.
You're just pathetic! But
I say your views don't carry
any weight. She'll marry
quality. It's feasible
to reach Marquise,
and so she will. And if
you try again to miff
me like you do, I warn
you, I'll see that her spouse
is even more high born,
and not one of your lousy
common types. So there!

[EXIT JOURDAIN]

MADAME JOURDAIN:
So help me—! Don't despair,
Cléonte. Come on, Lucile!
We'll get around him yet.
You've only got to steel

yourself, say you're dead set
against him. If you can't
have Cléonte, then you shan't
have anyone.

[EXEUNT MADAME JOURDAIN,
LUCILE AND NICOLE]

COVIELLE: Hey, Boss,
with great respect, you cocked
it up. Why did you cross
him when you should have socked
it to him straight? "A gentleman?
Of course I am!"
Why be so reticent?
Just go for the grand slam.
You've got to do or die:
no harm in a white lie.

CLÉONTE: For me, the principle's
the thing that matters
most. I could get in
with him of course by flattering
his folly.

COVIELLE: Well,
why didn't you?

CLÉONTE: What? Tell
a blatant lie? I'd sooner
not have him dragoon
me into standing down
whenever my renowned
ancestry proved a myth.
My Dad was a blacksmith!

[COVIELLE BURSTS OUT LAUGHING]
What's funny about that?

COVIELLE: No, something else. I've just
seen an aristocrat
in my mind's eye.

CLÉONTE: What?

COVIELLE: Trust
me, Boss. I've got a great
idea. Just you wait!

[BLACKOUT]

[LIGHTS. MUSIC MASTER'S
PUPIL IS SEEN COMPOSING
MUSIC. ENTER MUSIC MASTER
AND DANCING MASTER,
DEEP IN CONVERSATION]

MUSIC MASTER [TO PUPIL]:
Have you finished your task?

[MUSIC MASTER'S PUPIL HANDS
HIM THE MUSIC]

DANCING MASTER: What's that?

MUSIC MASTER: Something I asked
him to write—a new song.
[HE INSPECTS THE MUSIC]
Good! That's coming along
rather nicely—except
that F-sharp. That's inept.
Look, it makes a tritone.

Use an A like I've shown
you before.

DANCING MASTER: May we hear
it?

MUSIC MASTER: When Jourdain appears.
He's due back here soon, is
he not?

DANCING MASTER: We're keeping busy
these days. That's good news.

MUSIC MASTER: Thanks to Jourdain's enthusiasm
for acquiring
new skills and aspiring
to greater facility
in things artistic,
to greater finesse.
He may think the nobility
wax eulogistic
at such false noblesse,
but as long as he's learning
from us, we are earning
an excellent living.

DANCING MASTER: I have some misgivings
on that score. My teaching
is sadly not reaching
the parts of his brain
I'm supposed to be training.
I'll grant you he's willing
but it's not fulfilling
to have to teach dance
to a pupil who prances

about off the beat
with a pair of left feet.

MUSIC MASTER: He's not terribly gifted,
it's true, but our wages
are not to be sniffed
at. The money assuages
one's lack of fulfilment.
It is the distilment
of our years of clever
artistic endeavour.
Do you not like banking
all those lovely francs?

DANCING MASTER: Huh! It's far too simplistic
to speak of artistic
endeavour in terms
such as you seem so firmly
attached to. I say
that the only true pay
for an artist's applause.
Without that we've no cause
for fulfilment. And it's
just the absolute pits
to be casting one's pearls
before ignorant churls
who would not know true grace
if it flew in their face.
You can say what you like
but I know that the psyche
of any musician
depends for nutrition
on due recognition,
from being embraced
by discerning good taste.

MUSIC MASTER: That's a neat turn of phrase!
That may be, and yet praise
alone isn't enough.
Praise does not pay the bills.
The best praise is the stuff
that he gives us that fills
up our wallets. He mightn't
be the most enlightened
of men, but his money
flows like runny honey.
Is that not acclaim
by as honest a name?

DANCING MASTER: Maybe, but I'd say
that—Look sharp.

[ENTER JOURDAIN,
DRESSED IN HIS NEW SUIT]

JOURDAIN: Good day,
Messieurs! Have you some play-
acting thingies to show?

DANCING MASTER: Thingies?

MUSIC MASTER: Play-acting?

DANCING MASTER: No!

JOURDAIN: But I thought you were bringing—
you know, people flinging
their bodies and pinging
their instruments.

MUSIC MASTER: Singing
and dancing?

JOURDAIN: That's it,
yes! I find it a bit
hard to get a firm grip
on the technical words.
They were just on the tip
of my tongue when I heard
you repeat them by chance.
Yes, yes, singing and dancing,
of course! So! At last
here I am. Had that blasted
man not been so late
coming, keeping me waiting
for ages, I ought
to have been here. He brought
me this fine new suit. Elegant,
eh? And how well
it becomes me. I dress
pretty splendidly, don't
you agree?

MUSIC MASTER: Indeed!

DANCING MASTER: Yes!

JOURDAIN: That's real quality. Won't
everyone be impressed?

DANCING MASTER: No doubt!

MUSIC MASTER: Monsieur knows best.

JOURDAIN: The erotic brocade
was especially made
for me. Look at that! Pure
Chinese silk.

MUSIC MASTER: Yes, Monsieur.

JOURDAIN [CALLING]: Lackey!

LACKEY [APPEARING AS IF BY MAGIC]:
Monsieur?

JOURDAIN: Go! [LACKEY VANISHES] I
just thought I ought to try
exercising my forceful
command voice.

MUSIC MASTER: Of course,
Monsieur.

JOURDAIN: So we're agreed
I look good?

MUSIC MASTER: Yes.

DANCING MASTER: Indeed!

MUSIC MASTER: You look splendid.

JOURDAIN: Right! So!
Let's get on with your show.

MUSIC MASTER: Yes, Monsieur. Now, we are
in luck, Monsieur. My star
pupil—he over there—
gives the world première
of "Lament II", his latest
new piece.

JOURDAIN: No, no! Wait!
Why *his* piece? Why not your
piece, you lazy man? Surely

you don't think I'm willing
to have you go filling
your pockets and shirking?
You're meant to be working
for me, Sir, not robbing
me, Sir, and then fobbing
me off with some second
rate rot.

MUSIC MASTER: But so fecund
is his creativity
that you must give
him a hearing. I said
he's a pupil. The truth
is I may have misled
you. In spite of his youth
he's a real up-and-coming
artiste. You'll be humming
his music before
long and asking for more.

JOURDAIN: I suppose maybe I
ought to give it a try.

MUSIC MASTER: Thank you, Monsieur! I knew
you'd see sense.
[ANNOUNCING THE PIECE] "Lament II".

MUSIC MASTER'S PUPIL
[SINGING AND PLAYING]:
Fie on all unloving love that heartless rends
my heart in twain and fills me full of deepest woes.
Fair Iris, if thus cruelly you treat your friends,
I shudder to imagine how you treat your foes.

MUSIC MASTER: When it comes to melisma
he is a true master.

JOURDAIN: But it was so dismal.
Could it not be faster?
I struggled to keep
me from falling asleep.

MUSIC MASTER: But the music must fit
the words.

JOURDAIN: I learned a little
song once, a lot happier,
and a lot snappier.
[TRYING TO REMEMBER] How did it go?

DANCING MASTER: But Sir, how should I know?

JOURDAIN: No, no, just wait a minute—
there was a sheep in it.

MUSIC MASTER: A sheep?

JOURDAIN: No, a ram.

DANCING MASTER: A ram?

JOURDAIN: That's it: a lamb.
[SINGS] "I thought my lovely Jane as sweet
a girl as you could hope to meet—
So fair of face, so kind, as meek
as any lamb—Until last week
when I fell foul of her abuse—
Now she's a tiger on the loose."
Is that not a nice ditty?
It's certainly prettier
than your depressing
old dirge.

MUSIC MASTER: Maybe—yes.

DANCING MASTER: Your unusual style
gives one something to smile
at.

JOURDAIN: And yet no one's taught
me to sing.

MUSIC MASTER: But you ought
to learn music. The best
people do.

JOURDAIN: Do they, now?

MUSIC MASTER: They take great interest
in it.

JOURDAIN: Then I'll allow
you to teach me. But still,
I don't know if I will
have the time: there's my fencing,
and I'm just commencing
a course in philosophy.
How can I possibly
fit it all in?
I'll be spread a bit thin,
won't I?

MUSIC MASTER: Take it from me,
Monsieur, philosophy
does of course play its part,
but the consummate art
form is music.

DANCING MASTER: And dancing!
It's so life-enhancing.

MUSIC MASTER: The life of the nation,
all civilisation's
completely dependent
on music to tend
and to care for its soul.

DANCING MASTER: And consider the rôle
dancing's played in the progress
of social development.
How could we grow,
as a race, into well
rounded people without
it? We would be a gout-ridden
species of slobs.

JOURDAIN: You'd be out of your jobs
for a start!

MUSIC MASTER: Human strife
is what comes of a life
without music.

DANCING MASTER: Mischance
falls on those who can't dance.

JOURDAIN: How so?

MUSIC MASTER: Strife is discord,
is it not?

JOURDAIN: Yes?

MUSIC MASTER: But we
find, through good music, order
and true harmony.

DANCING MASTER: And when somebody makes
an unhappy mistake,
people say that he's put
a foot wrong. That same foot
might be put right if he
had learned dancing.

JOURDAIN: I see.

MUSIC MASTER: But Monsieur has not heard
the new work we've prepared
in his honour. I trust
he would like—?

JOURDAIN [BORED]: If I must!

MUSIC MASTER: Thank you!

DANCING MASTER: Here is my corps
de ballet. Please ignore
their fine clothes. That's a shepherd,
intended to represent
life in Arcadia.

JOURDAIN: Hm! And the lady?

DANCING MASTER: A nymph!

JOURDAIN: Every time
it's the same. Tell me, why
is it always a shepherd?
Why not have a—leopard,
or something exciting
like that in your writing?
Are shepherds the best
you can do? You're obsessed!

MUSIC MASTER: It's artistic convention,
that's all.

DANCING MASTER: Our intention's
to tell out a story
in deep, allegorical
terms.

MUSIC MASTER: So the plot
doesn't matter a jot.

DANCING MASTER: And one may not omit
to—

JOURDAIN: Oh, get on with it!

[A MASQUE FOR DANCING,
PERFORMED BY A SHEPHERD, A
NYMPH AND SEVERAL SHEEP]

DANCING MASTER:
Behold! A shepherd stands, keeping his sheep—
Until, feeling drowsy, he falleth asleep—
Seeing his plight his sheep weepeth sad tears—
He sleepeth on for a hundred-odd years—
Cometh a nymph, waketh him with a kiss—
Soon be they wedded, O rapture and bliss!

JOURDAIN: Was that it?

DANCING MASTER: Yes!

JOURDAIN: How thrilling!
[LAUGHING UPROARIOUSLY]
The sheep! They were *killing*!
[REGAINING HIS COMPOSURE]

Right! Pack it away.
That's enough for today.

[EXEUNT ALL EXCEPT JOURDAIN. ENTER DORANTE, SMILING OBSEQUIOUSLY]

DORANTE: Jourdain, dear friend, how goes it?

JOURDAIN [WELCOMING HIM]: Wait! I'll close the door for privacy.
I don't think we
want my dear wife to share
our plan.
[HE CLOSES THE DOOR] Good! There we are! I'm very well.
And you, dear fellow?
How are things?

DORANTE: Why, splendid,
my dear friend!
And Madame J?

MADAME JOURDAIN [APPEARING SUDDENLY]: She's frightfully all right.
thank you.

DORANTE: Madame! How charming!

JOURDAIN [ASIDE]: Huh! Alarming,
I would say.

MADAME JOURDAIN: What, dear?

JOURDAIN: Leave us.

MADAME JOURDAIN: No fear!

DORANTE: Your dress sense is impeccable,
old man!
There's no one by my reckoning
who can
surpass you, Sir. You set
so high a standard
as to pose a threat
to all those fusty
socialites.
You're all the talk! "Why must
that Jourdain dress in quite
so avant garde a way?"
They know that they
do not come up to scratch.
Nor can they match
so great a paradigm.

MADAME JOURDAIN [ASIDE]: Oh, what a slimy
slug!

DORANTE: Turn round!
[JOURDAIN PIROUETTES] Oh, wow!
I don't know how
you do it.

MADAME JOURDAIN [ASIDE]: Yes indeed.
You'd not thought he'd
look stupid from behind
as well.

DORANTE: I find
your company no less

great than your dress
sense. Such is my esteem
for you I seem
unable to forgo
the slightest chance,
Sir, to advance
your cause. I'd have you know
this very morning I
was talking to His Highness
about you.

JOURDAIN: Dear friend, you do
me too much honour.
[ASIDE, TO MADAME JOURDAIN] Hark
at that remark,
eh!

DORANTE: Come, Sir, not a whit!
No honour done
to someone so hospitable
is undeserved.

JOURDAIN: For this great kindness
I'm indebted
to you.

DORANTE: No, Sir, let
me please remind
you: it is I who owe
you!

MADAME JOURDAIN: Don't we know
it!

JOURDAIN: Sir, don't speak of that!

MADAME JOURDAIN: Shut up, you prat!
Don't let him get away
with it.

DORANTE: I'll say
it, Sir. It must be said.
It would be dreadful
if I just pretended
that your friendship
has been less than wonderful.
I'm under
no small obligation
to you. You've
done much to prove
your great consideration.
That alone has meant
a lot to me.
The fact that you have lent
your money freely
caps it all. You are
a shining star
of generosity.

JOURDAIN [FALSE MODESTY]: No, no!

DORANTE: Let me
continue! As I value
that, I shall
repay you every penny.
How could any
decent man do less?
Let us assess
the debt, so that I may
arrange to pay
in full.

JOURDAIN [ASIDE, TO MADAME JOURDAIN]:
See who was right?
You and your spiteful
tongue!

DORANTE: I pay my way.

JOURDAIN: What did I say?
See now!

DORANTE: So, shall we add
things up?

JOURDAIN: You're badly
wrong, the way you judge
him. You begrudge
the man his decency.

DORANTE: Let's see if we
can tally the amounts
on my account.
No doubt you've kept a note?

JOURDAIN: I'm sure I wrote
things down.
[WITH INDECENT HASTE, HE
PRODUCES A LONG ROLL OF PAPER]
Ah yes, I've found
it. The two hundred pounds
was first.

DORANTE: Agreed.

JOURDAIN: And then you needed
sixty-five pounds more.

DORANTE: That's right.

JOURDAIN: Then four
small lots of forty-six
pounds.

DORANTE: Your arithmetic's
exact, Sir.

JOURDAIN: We
then paid the three
outstanding clothing bills.

DORANTE: Just so! We're still
agreed.

JOURDAIN: And then
the three-hundred-and-ten
pound bill for stabling fees.

DORANTE: That's right.

JOURDAIN: Then these
six lots of ten.

DORANTE: Correct.

JOURDAIN: That's it. We've checked
them all.

DORANTE: Your sums match mine.

JOURDAIN: I make it nine-
six-two in total.

DORANTE: Spot
on! If you've got

another hundred you
can spare today,
that makes one-o-six-two
pounds I shall pay
back at the very first
chance.

MADAME JOURDAIN: Think the worst
of decent folk, do I?
The man's as sly
as fifty foxes.

JOURDAIN: Shut
it, woman!

DORANTE: But
if it is inconvenient—?

JOURDAIN: No—

MADAME JOURDAIN: You mean
you're going to let him kid
you still. You idiot!

JOURDAIN: Be silent!

DORANTE: Please,
if it's not easy
for you, I can always
go and call
on someone else.

JOURDAIN: No, wait!

MADAME JOURDAIN: He's got you hooked.
You can't resist the bait.

JOURDAIN: So help me!
[TO MADAME JOURDAIN] Look,
you, not another word.

DORANTE: Dear friend! Good Sir!
Don't worry if you can't
oblige. I shan't
have any trouble finding
others kind
enough to want to lend
to me—as long
as that's not wrong
by you. You'd be offended,
though, I know, if I
should pass you by
in such a way. That's why
I've come to see you first.

JOURDAIN: I'll fetch my purse.

MADAME JOURDAIN: Don't do it. You're a fool!
Look at him, cool
as anything. He means
to strip you clean,
sunshine.

JOURDAIN: I can't refuse
somebody who's
been visiting the King
and mentioning
my name.

MADAME JOURDAIN: Go on, then, stump
up. Let him pump
you dry, and watch him dump
you, stupid chump!

[EXIT JOURDAIN]

DORANTE: Madame, are you unwell?

MADAME JOURDAIN: I'm more intelligent
than your dear, gullible
numskull,
that's all.

DORANTE: Your daughter, is
she well?

MADAME JOURDAIN: Don't quiz
me about her. I'll see
to it that she
keeps well out of your clutches.

DORANTE: She is such a
splendid girl. I daresay
that you were
once equally attractive—
I mean back
in younger days.

MADAME JOURDAIN: So I'm
well past my prime,
you reckon?

DORANTE: I've upset
you. How regrettable!
I was forgetting
how—er, young you are.
I beg your pardon!

JOURDAIN [RETURNING AND HANDING
OVER THE MONEY]:
So, one hundred pounds!

DORANTE: Sir, your astounding
kindness leaves me speechless.
I beseech
you, if at court you seek
some favour, speak
it: if my influence
can recompense
your kindness in the slightest,
I'll delight
in using it on your
behalf.

JOURDAIN: I'm sure.

DORANTE: Madame need only ask
to see a masque
at court, and she'll be treated
to a seat
right up in the front row.

MADAME JOURDAIN: Madame says no
thanks very much.

DORANTE [ASIDE, TO JOURDAIN]: A private
word, Sir. I've
succeeded in persuading
the good lady
You-Know-Who to overcome
her slowness
to accept you. She
has finally
permitted me to say
that she will dine
here and see the ballet

with us, at nine
tonight.

JOURDAIN: Let's walk this way
a bit. I rather fear
that old Big Ears
is still tuned in. [PAUSE, UNTIL OUT OF EARSHOT] The diamond
that I
gave you to give her as
a present—has
it made the right impression?

DORANTE: Her discretion
almost got the better,
but she let
herself take my advice.
I said how nice
a chap you were, and thoughtful,
that she ought
to see it as a token
of unspoken
admiration, whereupon
she carefully
deposited
it in her jewel
box.

JOURDAIN: And has it led
to some improvement
in my chances?

DORANTE: I'd
say if you bide

your time, she'll see the light;
you'll be all right.

JOURDAIN: I wish!

[ENTER NICOLE,
UNNOTICED BY THE MEN]

NICOLE [TO MADAME JOURDAIN]:
I see Bloodsucker
Bill is stuck
on him again.

JOURDAIN: I'm touched
that you do such
good work on my behalf.

NICOLE: He's such a crafty
devil.

DORANTE: I extend
our bond of friendship
further, that is all.
I do but small
things any friend would do.
I'm sure that you
would do the same for me.

JOURDAIN: Of course!

NICOLE: He wheedles
his way in, then digs
his claws deep, plays
upon his victim's ignorance
and stays
there, clinging limpet-like.

DORANTE: I think you're striking
just the very chord.
There is no more
decisive way to win
her heart than in
the way you're doing, lavishing
your ravishing
largess on her.
There's nothing stirs
a woman's base instincts
like when she thinks
she's having money spent
on her. Your sentimental
serenades,
the firework display,
the silk brocade,
all those bouquets,
the diamond, this dinner,
the ballet:
if anything will win
her, these will.

JOURDAIN: Maybe
so! I'd willingly
spend two or three
times more if it would buy
me such a high
born woman's love.

MADAME JOURDAIN: Just look
at them. They're cooking
up some plot, I'll swear.
Sneak over there
and see if you can eavesdrop.

[NICOLE MOVES CLOSER
TO THE MEN]

DORANTE: You'll achieve
some progress here tonight.
She'll be there, right
beside you at your table.

JOURDAIN: I've been able
to arrange it so
that my wife's going
to her sister's.

DORANTE: Good!
That was most prudent
of you. I have looked
in on the cook.
I've summoned the performers
to a warm-up
session in good time
for dinner. I'm
assured that every detail
is completely
in control.

JOURDAIN [NOTICING NICOLE]: What's this?
The servant's listening.
Come—We'd best get out.
Let's take a walk
outside and talk
where we can be alone.

[EXEUNT JOURDAIN AND
DORANTE]

NICOLE: I might have known
it. There's some scheme afoot.
I wouldn't put
it past them.

MADAME JOURDAIN: I'd say there's
a love affair
afoot. I know that leery
look. I fear
he'll come a cropper though.
Just wait! I'll show
him up without a doubt
before the day is out.

[EXEUNT MADAME JOURDAIN AND NICOLE. BLACKOUT]

[INTERVAL]

[LIGHTS. JOURDAIN
RETREATING FROM HIS WIFE]

JOURDAIN [CALLING BEHIND HIM]:
Don't think that you can bawl
me out in front of all
my friends and get
away with it.
I'll fix you yet.
[TO HIMSELF] I'm going to hit
her one of these days; treating
me like some deceitful
layabout. I'll beat
her black and blue,
like any gentleman
would do
to a dissenting
wife, show her who's boss.
[CALLING AGAIN] I mean it!
[TO HIMSELF AGAIN] I'm so cross.

[ENTER COVIELLE, DISGUISED]

COVIELLE: Monsieur, excuse
a total stranger
bringing news.
May we exchange
a few words?

JOURDAIN: Certainly,
but are you sure it's me
you—?

COVIELLE: Your identity
I know for sure.

I was a great
old friend of your
Papa, the late
lamented Jourdain,
the most eminent
of all the many gentlemen
I knew.

JOURDAIN: Lamented?
The most eminent?

COVIELLE: The same.
A very gem
for whom the name
of gentleman was no
match, far too low
an accolade.

JOURDAIN: But people say
he was a tradesman.

COVIELLE: What do they
know? He? A tradesman? Never!
No! He was a clever
man; that's why
these stupid people
like to try
their best to keep
the good man down. The fact
is that he always acted
out of kindness
for his friends.
He was inclined
to condescend

to help his friends by using
his great skill in choosing
textiles for
them and acquiring
them and storing
them, desiring
all his friends to see
his lovely cloth, and he
would give it to them freely—
Well, for a small fee.

JOURDAIN: I'm very glad
we've met at last.
I knew that Dad
was not the ghastly
salesman they maintain.
I hope you'll make that plain
to everyone.
Then they'll relent
and say his son
is a true gentleman.

COVIELLE: Yes—no mistake.
The more so when I break
my news.

JOURDAIN: Ah, yes?

COVIELLE: For years I have
been an obsessive
foreign traveller
in distant lands.
I've learned to understand
so many different

languages
by now that, if
somebody says
something to me in Greek
or Turkish, I can speak
right back.

JOURDAIN: My word!

COVIELLE: I've just returned
from my sojourn,
and when I heard
the Grand Turk's son's in town
I thought I'd toddle down
and have a chat.

JOURDAIN: The Grand Turk's son?
Well, fancy that!

COVIELLE: He has a hundred
servants.

JOURDAIN: Goodness gracious!

COVIELLE: The most ostentatious
clothes you ever
saw.

JOURDAIN: No? Bless
me! Well I never
did!

COVIELLE: And guess
what: he has just decided
who's to be his bride.

JOURDAIN: Who, then?

COVIELLE: Your lovely
daughter.

JOURDAIN: Really?
Heavens above!
You mean Lucile's
to wed the Grand Turk's son?
I'm absolutely stunned.

COVIELLE: How everyone
will stand in awe.
The Grand Turk's son:
your son-in-law.

JOURDAIN: My son-in-law.

COVIELLE: I went
to see him and we spent
some time in conversation
since
he looked upon
me, as these princes
do, with admiration
for my intonation
of his mother
tongue. Accordingly
he smothered
me with lordly
and fine-spirited
good wishes, and then said:
"Acciam croc soler ouch alla moustaph gidelum
amanahem varahini oussere carbulath",
which means: "Sir, has

it been your privilege
to meet a dazzling
lady said to live
here in Paree,
the daughter of the great
Jourdain, of celebrated
magnanimity?"

JOURDAIN: Did he say that?

COVIELLE: He did!

JOURDAIN: Oh my!
How very flattering!

COVIELLE: When I
told him I knew you well—
also Mademoiselle
Lucile—the great man fell
upon his knees
and bowed his head,
and in a wheezing
voice he said:
"Marababa Sahem",
which means: "My gentle dove,
I am consumed with love
for you".

JOURDAIN: For you?

COVIELLE: No, no, for her.
He said it to
me, but referred
to her. That's just a quirk
of modern spoken Turkish.

JOURDAIN: Who'd have thought
of such a thing?
To think my daughter
has him flinging
himself on his knees
and wheezing, before he's
as much as seen
her.

COVIELLE: So he's naturally
keen
to have a chat
and to gain your consent,
so much that he's intent
on coming round
this way to see
the much renowned
Jourdain.

JOURDAIN: Who? Me?

COVIELLE: Who else? He has suggested
that it's vital
that you be invested
with a title
of great honour such
that, while you may not touch
such rank as bears a crown,
you'll be the next one down.
By his decree
you are to be
Mamamouchi.
That is, as we
would say, a Paladin.

The Paladins were in
the olden days
the former—Paladins.

JOURDAIN: Amazing!

COVIELLE: So you shall
be of most noble rank.

JOURDAIN: My goodness! I must thank
him.

COVIELLE: Very soon
indeed, I'm sure.
Tomorrow noon: investiture,
then nuptials.

JOURDAIN: It's a trifle
sudden!

COVIELLE: You can't stifle
a true Turk's
love. They get straight
on with their work.
They really hate
delays of any kind. [LEAVING] Prepare:
tomorrow noon!

[EXIT COVIELLE]

JOURDAIN [CALLING AFTER HIM]:
What shall I wear?
[HE BREAKS INTO A DANCE. ENTER
MUSIC AND DANCING MASTERS]
Tomorrow I'll be
The Great Mamamouchi.

I'll be like royalty,
The Great Mamamouchi.
Oh, just think: little me,
The Great Mamamouchi.

DANCING MASTER [COACHING JOURDAIN]:
Good! Now *dance* with the *beat*.
Tap the *time* with your *feet*.
Two, three, *one*, two, three, *one*,
The Great *Ma*mamou*chi*.
Close the *mouth*. Raise the *chin*.
Shoulders *back*. Tummy *in*.
Two, three, *one*, two, three, *one*,
The Great *Ma*mamou*chi*.
Last one. *Fling* arms out *wide*.
Spin round. *That's* it. Well *tried*.
Two, three, *one*, two, three, *one*,
The Great *Ma*mamou*chi*.
[THE DANCE ENDS] Excellent! Excellent!

JOURDAIN [OUT OF BREATH]:
That reminds me. I meant
to ask you: show me how
does a gentlemen bow
to a countess he's not
met before, if he's got
some such meeting in mind.

DANCING MASTER: Yes, if you'll be so kind
as to give me your hand.

JOURDAIN: No, I'm happy to stand
watching you while you do it.

DANCING MASTER: But—

JOURDAIN: No buts! Jump to it!

DANCING MASTER: First, stand fully erect
as a mark of respect.
Three steps back. Then three slower
steps up, bowing lower
each time, with bow three
going down to her knee.

JOURDAIN: Well, then? Let's see you try.
[DANCING MASTER OBLIGES]
It's as easy as pie!

[ENTER LACKEY]

LACKEY: Monsieur, your fencing master's
here.

JOURDAIN: Send him in.
[LACKEY TURNS TO GO] Faster!

[ENTER FENCING MASTER.
HE GIVES A FOIL TO JOURDAIN,
AND STANDS WITH HIS OWN
FOIL VERTICALLY IN FRONT OF
HIS FACE. JOURDAIN IS MEANT
TO FOLLOW SUIT, BUT FAILS
TO DO SO]

FENCING MASTER: Come, let's have your salute.
Good! Now, do as your tutor
does. Back straight. Head high.
Try to let your left thigh
take the weight. Legs are fine
like that. Feet more in line.

Wrist down there by your hip.
And remember, the tip
of your foil at the height
of your shoulder. Arm slightly
more bent. Left hand there
at eye level. And square
up the shoulder. That's fairly
good. Head up. Strong glance.
Now, get set to advance.
Body steady. Engage,
and then lunge. Count the stages:
one, two. Now draw back
and repeat the attack.
Feet firm. One, two. Away!
It's a rule of sword-play
that the foil be withdrawn
first, or else there's a yawning
gap in one's defence.
One, two. Arm was not tense
enough that time. Hold hard.
Ready: one two. [FENCING MASTER
SCORES A FEW HITS]
En garde!
En garde!

[JOURDAIN GIVES UP AND
HANDS BACK THE FOIL]

JOURDAIN: Phew! Gracious me!

MUSIC MASTER: Well, you did splendidly.

FENCING MASTER: As I've told you, the whole
art of sword-play lies solely

in two things, to wit:
in delivering a hit,
and not taking one. Nor
need it take any more
than a flick of the wrist
to deflect or resist
any hit. Application
of this simple principle
makes one invincible.
My demonstration
last week made this clear.

JOURDAIN: So, then, it would appear
one is able to kill
someone else and yet still
be a coward.

FENCING MASTER: Correct!
That is why great respect
must be paid to good swordsmen.
You'd quickly get bored
if you should substitute
airy-fairy pursuits
such as music and dance
for your fencing.

DANCING MASTER: Don't chance
your arm too far, stick-shaker.

MUSIC MASTER: You're stupid.

DANCING MASTER: You make
an inordinate noise,
as if playing with toys
like that—thing was as gainful

as using your brain
like an artist.

FENCING MASTER: How dare
you attempt to compare
your professions with mine.

DANCING MASTER: You're a rank philistine.

MUSIC MASTER: You're a fine one to mock,
togged up like a great cockroach.

FENCING MASTER: My dear little fellow,
I could make you bellow
your music full blast.
As for you, Dancing Master,
I'd soon set you squealing
and dancing a reel
all at once.

MUSIC MASTER: Brainless twerp!

DANCING MASTER: Don't think you can usurp
intellectualists
with a flick of the wrist.
You can make a man bleed
but you can't make him heed
you, you authoritarian,
vulgar barbarian.

JOURDAIN: How can you brawl
with a man who knows all
about sword-play and fighting?
I hope you're not biting
off too much to chew.

MUSIC MASTER: Huh! He's long overdue
for a good talking to!

[FENCING MASTER SWIPES THE OTHERS, BUT THEY MANAGE TO DODGE HIM]

FENCING MASTER: Watch yourself, you
impertinent
fool.

DANCING MASTER: You stuffed shirt!

JOURDAIN: Masters, please!

MUSIC MASTER: Oaf!

DANCING MASTER: Buffoon!

MUSIC MASTER: Flapping windbag!

FENCING MASTER: Poltroon!

DANCING MASTER: Useless lump of old dross!

[ENTER PHILOSOPHY MASTER]

JOURDAIN: Ah, here's Mr Philosopher,
just in the nick
of time. Monsieur, come quickly
and help me prevent
any more argument.

PHILOSOPHY MASTER:
So? What have they been doing?

JOURDAIN: They've been bally-hooing
about their professions.

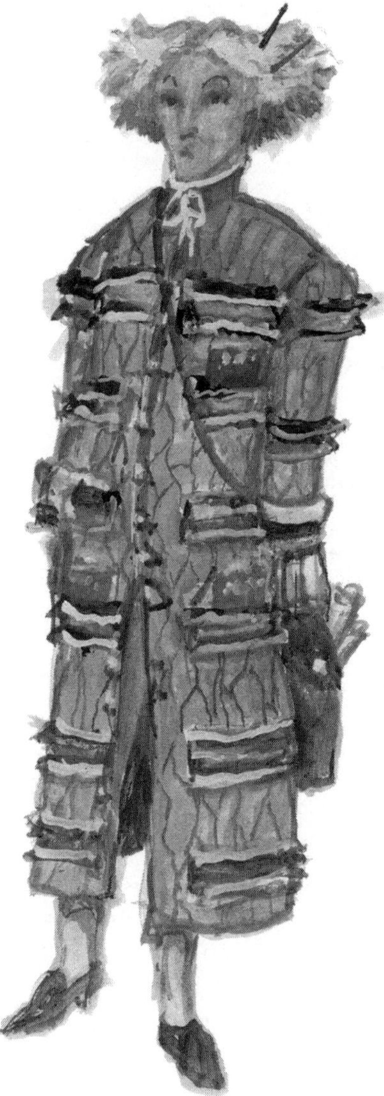

Each gives the impression
that nobody's is
as important as his.
I'm not sure that they will
be contented until
they've succeeded in killing
each other.

PHILOSOPHY MASTER: Come, come,
gentlemen. Must you plumb
the dark depths of your id?
Does not Seneca bid
us control our instincts
by the process of thinking?
He says in his treatise
on wrath, the elitist
position of man
with respect to mere animals
comes from superior
reason, yet here we are
fighting like cats!

DANCING MASTER: But you see, Monsieur, that's
the whole point: he's a beast!
He has not got the least
empathy for the arts,
such as set men apart
from the endless procession
of naked aggression
that is the hallmark
of the average shark.

PHILOSOPHY MASTER:
But the wise man knows better
than ever to let

a behaviour so bestial
pierce his celestial
armour. One ought
to let logical thought
be one's weapon of choice.
Rather than giving voice
to one's wrath, one should exercise
calm, disannex
one's instinctive reaction—
to seek satisfaction—
from one's higher sense.
Better calm sapience
than ill-judged vehemence.
A wise man's best defence
is his own eloquence,
not the malevolence
of his id.

FENCING MASTER: They saw fit
to declare that their pitiful
skills should be rated
with my elevated
abilities.

PHILOSOPHY MASTER: Why
should that cause you to fly
off the handle? You ought
to know that there is naught
to be gained from your obdurate,
unthinking squabble.
This fuss about rank
is vainglorious, frankly.
True precedence is
governed only by wisdom
and virtue.

DANCING MASTER: I still
think that dancing's a skill
worthy of the utmost
honour.

MUSIC MASTER: Music can boast
centuries of acclaim.

FENCING MASTER: But it's meaningless, aimless.
[TO JOURDAIN] These fools are both wrong.
As I've said all along,
swordsmanship's in a class
of its own, unsurpassed
in technique and invention.

PHILOSOPHY MASTER:
But you've failed to mention
philosophy, though
you must surely all know
that beside it the processes
that you describe
in your dull diatribe
are but base, meretricious
pursuits of fictitious
import. I'm appalled
that you rate your so-called
arts and crafts on a par
with philosophy. Are
you so utterly blinkered
that you think a thinker
does not, in his quest
for true meaning, attest
the true meaning of man?
That is far greater than

being, like you:
[TO MUSIC MASTER] troubadour,
[TO DANCING MASTER] exhibitionist, or
[TO FENCING MASTER] hempen hit-man.

FENCING MASTER: Be off
with you out of here, toffee-
nosed git!

MUSIC MASTER: You great smarty-
pants.

DANCING MASTER: Pompous upstart.

PHILOSOPHY MASTER:
Call me names, would you? Come
on then, miserable scum.
Stupid subjectivists.
Settle this with your fists.

[A FIST FIGHT ENSUES]

JOURDAIN: I say! Mr Philosopher!

PHILOSOPHY MASTER: Brainless misosophers.

MUSIC MASTER: Fix him, lads.

FENCING MASTER: Ouch!

JOURDAIN: Gentlemen!

PHILOSOPHY MASTER: Scaramouch!

DANCING MASTER: Dog!

MUSIC MASTER: Let's get him outside
and give him a good hiding.

[EXEUNT THE FOUR MASTERS]

JOURDAIN: Go on, do your worst!
Don't expect me to burst
a blood vessel umpiring.
[CALLING OFFSTAGE]
I'm thinking of firing
the lot of you. Don't
you imagine I won't!
[TO HIMSELF AGAIN] Anyway, I might soil
my perruke or else spoil
my brand new dressing gown.
Come, old man, let's sit down.

[BLACKOUT]

[LIGHTS. ENTER LACKEY,
LEADING DORANTE
AND DORIMÈNE.
JOURDAIN IS NOT ON STAGE]

LACKEY: The master bids me say
that he is on his way.
Will it please you to stay
in here?

DORANTE: That's good.

[EXIT LACKEY]

DORIMÈNE: Dorante, how could
you bring me to this place?
No one here knows my face.
It really is disgraceful
of you.

DORANTE: Since
you are convinced
we cannot meet at your
place or at mine, then surely
we must both endure
a rendezvous
that shelters you
from scandal.

DORIMÈNE: But you have
not mentioned the extravagances
that you lavish
on me daily,
as you gaily
seek to overpower
me: the way you shower
gifts on me—the flowers
and the fireworks,
this diamond
and now tonight's
as yet unseen delights.
You've clearly set your sights
on weakening
my wavering
resolve. You will not rest
until my vain protests
give way to your conquest.

DORANTE: And where's the harm
in that? You are
a widow, young, and free
to choose your destiny.
Say yes, and I will be
the happiest
of men.

DORIMÈNE: But best
be cautious. Marriage is
a very complex business
which can end in misery
unless
both sides possess
a most exacting range
of qualities. Exchanging
vows is fine. The danger
comes as soon
as honeymoon
time's over. Many people
find they cannot keep
alive the erstwhile, deep
affection that
they all too naturally
think will thrive
until their very lives'
end. So unless they strive
to love through thick
and thin, and stick
together down the years,
they may end up in tears.

DORANTE: But why must you appear
so negative?
Can't you forgive
the past? It seems the bad
experience you've had
has had an all too radical
effect
on your subjective
consciousness. But are

you justified in tarring
every single marriage
with the same
brush? No, for shame!

DORIMÈNE: But still my point remains:
the prodigal campaign
you're waging is constraining
my choice. It
seeks to commit
me further than I wish.
And is not all this swish
expense impoverishing
you? Don't get
yourself in debt
on my account.

DORANTE: These things
are tokens, trifles, trinkets,
and—

DORIMÈNE: The diamond ring?
A trinket? Nonsense,
that's dishonest!
Sir, you understate
its worth. It is the greatest—

DORANTE: Don't exaggerate
its worth, when it
is just a little
thing, beyond compare
with someone who's as fair
as you, Madame.
[ENTER JOURDAIN] But there

is our kind host.
Sir, I am most—

JOURDAIN [ATTEMPTING THE TRIPLE BOW]:
Please! Back a step or two,
Madame.

DORIMÈNE: What is he doing?

JOURDAIN: One more.

DORANTE: Paying due
respect.

JOURDAIN: And now
for my third bow.

DORANTE: Monsieur Jourdain is just
adhering to his customary
upper crust
behaviour, Madam.

JOURDAIN [TO DORIMÈNE]: I'm so glad
that you should be so civil
as to grant this privilege
to me of giving
me the honour
of—

DORANTE: Upon
my word, Monsieur, my lady
doesn't like being made
a fuss of.
[ASIDE TO DORIMÈNE] He's a tradesman,
rather gauche
and lacking social
skills.

DORIMÈNE [ASIDE TO DORANTE]:
That's evident.

DORANTE: Monsieur Jourdain's a gentleman
most eminent.

JOURDAIN: Monsieur, you're too
kind.

DORIMÈNE: I am truly
honoured.

JOURDAIN: It's a minor
honour for so fine
a lady.

DORANTE [TAKING JOURDAIN ASIDE]:
Sir, a tiny
word. Take care
not to refer
to it—you know—the diamond
you gave her.

JOURDAIN: Why not?

DORANTE: It would be a trifle
vulgar. Gentlemen
present
themselves in the most diffident
of terms, as if
their gifts were insignificant
effects
which they neglect
to mention. [THEY RETURN
TO DORIMÈNE] My old friend

was just saying how splendid
that you've condescended
to join in our
little dinner.

DORIMÈNE: I am so delighted
to have been invited
here, I'm sure.

JOURDAIN [ASIDE, TO DORANTE]: You're quite
adept, I'll say
that!

DORANTE [ASIDE, TO JOURDAIN]:
She was playing
hard to get, of course,
until my firm endorsement
of your standing forced
her to give way.
[TO DORIMÈNE] My friend was saying
how very agreeable
it is to be
in such sweet company.

DORIMÈNE: I'm deeply touched.
Monsieur is much
too kind.

DORANTE: The chef entreats
us please to take our seats.
It's time for us to eat.

JOURDAIN: Let there be music,
food and booze.

[THEY SIT AT TABLE.
ENTER MUSICIANS]

MUSICIANS: Let the fruits of all the earth
fill you and increase your girth.
Drink the wine for all you're worth,
wherefore make we merry mirth.

JOURDAIN: I hope you heard
them sing the words.
I wrote them.

DORIMÈNE: Did you really?

DORANTE: Such great depth of feeling!

DORIMÈNE: What a lovely meal!

JOURDAIN: Oh no, I fear
it can't come near
to your accustomed standards.

DORANTE: If Damis had planned
it, it would have been handled
to perfection.
Such selection
of ingredients!
Such fine accompaniments!
And then his great propensity
for holding
forth untold
delights to all his guests.
He would say that this breast
of duckling had been dressed
fit for the King

himself. He'd sing
the praises of the side-
salad, and he would guide
us to perceive the fried
potato chips
as craftsmanship
unequalled, eulogise
the sprouts and rhapsodise,
in the most appetising
terms, the sauce.
Without such awesome
powers of rhetoric
as his, it's politic
if I decide to stick
with Monsieur Jourdain's
line, demure
as it may be: the pity
is, I must admit
this meal is hardly fit,
nor yet the wine,
for one as fine
as you.

DORIMÈNE: But, as you see,
I eat most heartily,
for all my finery.

JOURDAIN: Your hands are poetry
in motion.

DORIMÈNE: I guess you're referring
to the diamond there:
a gemstone of the rarest
quality.

JOURDAIN: Good gracious me!
You don't think I would sully
myself with such vulgar
usage and uncultured
manners! Why,
I'd say the diamond
is just a paltry
thing.

DORIMÈNE: You've got exalted
taste.

JOURDAIN: Why, not at all!
Too kind, Ma'am!

DORANTE [CALLING A LACKEY]: Come,
more wine, and summon
our musicians.
[ENTER MUSICIANS]
Entertain
us with some gentle
strains of incidental
music.

DORIMÈNE: Marvellous!
We are
being entertained most admirably.
I'm so glad
I came.

JOURDAIN: Permit me, Madam—

DORANTE: Monsieur, please.
Silence for these
musicians. Their saltation

has more fascination
than our conversation.

MUSICIANS [MIMING WITH SUNG ACCOMPANIMENT]:
He treated her aggressively.
She held him too possessively.
They had it out impressively.
Now they're in love excessively.

DORIMÈNE: That's most disarming.

JOURDAIN [PUTTING HIS HAND ON HERS]:
Not as charming
as Madame, though, eh.

DORIMÈNE [WITHDRAWING HER HAND]:
Monsieur Jourdain, I say!
That was a bit risqué!

DORANTE: For pity's sake.
What do you take
him for!

JOURDAIN: I wish she would
take me.

DORANTE: Madame, how could
you! You've misunderstood
him.

JOURDAIN: She'll soon know
me better.

DORIMÈNE: Oh,
I give up!

[ENTER MADAME JOURDAIN]

MADAME JOURDAIN: Here's a cosy
little tête-a-tête.
[TO DORANTE]
I'm Monsieur Jourdain's nosy
wife, [TO JOURDAIN] lest he forget.
No wonder he
packed me off to my sister's.
Luckily
I stayed here. I'd have missed
a treat: downstairs a theatre,
here gluttony
on an appalling scale.
[TO JOURDAIN] Sir, this is a wholesale
affront. You use
our house like a bordel;
bring in your floosies
hoping they will sell
themselves for—

DORANTE [SHUTTING HER UP]:
Madam, please!
These wild hypotheses
are all unfounded.
You have rounded
on the wrong man. Save
your breath. 'Twas I who gave
the order for this feast
and summoned the artistes.
This lady is my guest.
She's here at my behest.
And your gallant
husband has granted

me the use of his
house. That is all there is
to say.

JOURDAIN [TO MADAME JOURDAIN]: There
now,
you silly cow.
Monsieur le Comte does us
much honour, but you treat
him in this scandalous
way. Madam, you're completely
wrong.

MADAME JOURDAIN: You can't believe
I could be that naive!

JOURDAIN: May I make my position—

MADAME JOURDAIN: I've had my suspicions
for a good long time.
[TO DORANTE] How very cruel
of you to
allow his social climbing.
Look at the expense!
Look at this decadence!
And as for
[TURNING TO DORIMÈNE] wots-yer-name,
you ought to be ashamed
to let yourself be framed
in this way, letting poor,
defenceless men think you're
available for rent
to any would-be gentleman.

DORIMÈNE: How dare
you, Madam!

[TO DORANTE] Spare
me from this vile,
insane reptile.

[EXEUNT DORANTE AND DORIMÈNE]

JOURDAIN [CALLING AFTER THEM]: Please,
Madam, wait!
Dorante! Too late.
[ROUNDING ON MADAME JOURDAIN]
So there! Was that what you
intended? Now you've ruined
me. Is that enough,
you traitress, you insufferable
slob!

MADAME JOURDAIN: Oh, shut your gob!

[EXEUNT MADAME JOURDAIN]

JOURDAIN [CALLING AFTER HER]:
I ought to smash this plate
across your face
for your disgraceful,
gross, infuriating—
I'll fix you all right.
Just keep out of my sight.

[BLACKOUT]

[LIGHTS. JOURDAIN AND PHILOSOPHY MASTER]

PHILOSOPHY MASTER: Now, Sir, shall we begin?

JOURDAIN: I'm so sorry they injured
you.

PHILOSOPHY MASTER: A wise man knows
how to deal with opposing
views. I shall fight back
with a ruthless attack
full of blood, guts and fire:
An incisive satire
after Juvenal. Well,
are you going to tell
me what you want to learn?

JOURDAIN: Above all, I've a burning
desire for knowledge.
I missed out on college.
I'm sure any -ology
you care to mention
would grab my attention.

PHILOSOPHY MASTER: That's most prescient.
Nam sine doctrina vita est quasi mortis imago.
You do know what is meant
by that?

JOURDAIN: Yes, but proceed
as if you thought I needed
to have it explained.

PHILOSOPHY MASTER:
Without knowledge we feign
death in life.

JOURDAIN: What you've said
hits the nail on the head.

PHILOSOPHY MASTER: Have you been inculcated
in matters related
to science?

JOURDAIN: Yes, quite!
I can both read and write.

PHILOSOPHY MASTER: Would you like
pedagogical
coaching in logic?

JOURDAIN: That does sound exquisite,
but tell me: what is it?

PHILOSOPHY MASTER: Logic will instruct
you in three ineluctable
patterns of thinking.

JOURDAIN: Go on! I'm all ears!

PHILOSOPHY MASTER: Pattern one is the linking
in mind of adherent
relationships. Two
is the act of construing
inclusion in categories.
The third pattern
is the perihelion:
Aristotelian
reasoning: syllogisation:
the skill
of deducing from binary
premises.

JOURDAIN: Fine,
but it sounds rather dull.

I'd as soon fill my skull
with—well—something less quarrelsome.

PHILOSOPHY MASTER: Something like moral
philosophy?

JOURDAIN: Just
remind me.

PHILOSOPHY MASTER: The broad thrust
of it is to instil
knowledge of self-fulfilment
and teach self-control
of emotion.

JOURDAIN: Sounds droll
enough. Nevertheless,
I don't think I should mess
with that. I like being cross,
and if moral philosophy
doesn't agree,
then it can't be for me.
[PAUSE]
Could you teach me to be
a great Mamamouchi?

PHILOSOPHY MASTER: Just remind
me.

JOURDAIN: It's kin
to a great Paladin.

PHILOSOPHY MASTER: I could discourse on rank.

JOURDAIN: Nice one! Most useful! Thanks!

PHILOSOPHY MASTER:

I reason that mankind's primordial
pursuit of pecking order
issues from his insecurity.
It takes outstanding purity
of thought to find obscurity
fulfilling. Our aspiring
nature, our innate desire
for recognition drive
our minds, and so we strive
to gain outstanding recognition.
Socially, that means position,
rank. In social hierarchy
based on wealth, the oligarchy
holds sway not because of merit
but material inheritance.
All those who fear exclusion
suffer under the delusion
that a higher social station
must mean greater approbation
and fulfilment. But the wise
man sees these things for foolish lies.
Wise men do not aspire
to rank, but something higher:
not material effect
but greater power of intellect.
Some simple words for those who seek to climb
the social ladder: you are losing time!

JOURDAIN: Huh! Now that's off your chest,
I've got one more request.
I was wondering, could you
do a short billet doux

for me. It's to a beautiful
woman.

PHILOSOPHY MASTER: Quite so.

JOURDAIN: I just want her to know
that I love her.

PHILOSOPHY MASTER: Right-o—
Would you like verse or prose?

JOURDAIN: No, no, not one of those!

PHILOSOPHY MASTER: But it has to be one
or the other.

JOURDAIN: Just run
me through that.

PHILOSOPHY MASTER: One composes
in verse, or else prose.
Anything that's not verse,
be it better or worse,
must be prose.

JOURDAIN: When I say
something like "Get away
with you, woman, and fetch
me my slippers", or "Ketchup
please, Missus", then I'm
talking prose?

PHILOSOPHY MASTER: Yes.

JOURDAIN: Well, blimey!
Stone me! All this time,
all these years talking prose

and I never supposed
I was. That's the most sensible
thing you've said yet.
Goodness me! [FUMBLES IN HIS POCKET
AND PULLS OUT A COIN] Here's six pence
for you. Now to the letter.
I want to design
me a note on these lines:
"Madame,
I am
so mesmerised
by your dark eyes,
I only crave
to be your slave."
But it's got to have feeling,
and must sound genteel.

PHILOSOPHY MASTER:
Well, perhaps if you told her
something like: her smouldering
glances have fired
your latent desire
so much that you pine—

JOURDAIN: But I want to use mine:
"Madame,
I am
so mesmerised
by your dark eyes,
I only crave
to be your slave."

PHILOSOPHY MASTER:
You want something more florid?

JOURDAIN: No, that would be horrid.
I just want precisely
my words, only nicely
arranged. Please recite
all the ways that I might
say the same thing, but using
my words, and I'll choose.

PHILOSOPHY MASTER:
Well, you might try this way:
"To be your slave
I only crave,
Madame,
so mesmerised
I am
by your dark eyes."
[JOURDAIN IS NON-COMMITTAL]
"I am
so mesmerised,
Madame,
by your dark eyes,
I only crave
to be your slave."
[PAUSE]
Then again you might say:
"By your dark eyes,
Madame,
so mesmerised
I am,
to be your slave
I only crave."

JOURDAIN: Which one would you suggest?

PHILOSOPHY MASTER: I'd say yours is the best:
"Madame,
I am
so mesmerised
by your dark eyes,
I only crave
to be your slave."

JOURDAIN: So you don't need to teach
me to write a good speech!
Thank you very much! Great,
then! Tomorrow at eight.
[EXIT PHILOSOPHY MASTER]
"Madame,
I am
so mesmerised
by your dark eyes,
I only crave
to be your slave."

[ENTER COVIELLE,
DISGUISED AS BEFORE]

COVIELLE: It's midday. Are you ready?

JOURDAIN: You know she's going steady
with someone unsuitable,
and she's immutable
in this respect,
and she's bound to object
to your master's grand plan.
She's obsessed with this man
called Cléonte.

COVIELLE: She'll discover
a new, better lover

whenever she sees
the Grand Turk's son. But he's
coming.
[ENTER CLÉONTE, DISGUISED,
WITH A RETINUE OF SERVANTS]
Quick, on your knees!

CLÉONTE: Ambousahim oqui boraf, Jordina!
Salamalequi!

COVIELLE: Which means, literally:
"May your heart be all year
like a flowering rose tree."
They like using these queer
forms of greeting, these royal
types.

JOURDAIN: I'm overjoyed!
Tell him I'm his most fervent
and most humble servant.

COVIELLE: Carigar camboto oustin moraf.

CLÉONTE: Oustin yoc catamalequi basum base alla
moran.

COVIELLE: His Highness was saying,
or should I say praying,
that Heaven endow
your good self with the prowess
of lions and wisdom
of serpents.

JOURDAIN: Tell his
esteemed Turkish Highness
that I wish him no less.

COVIELLE: Ossa binamin sadoc babally oracaf
ouram.

CLÉONTE: Bel men.

COVIELLE: He says, if you're agreed,
he would like to proceed
with the investiture
and, immediately you're
made a Mamamouchi,
with the ceremony
of the nuptials.

JOURDAIN: My hat!
Just two words to say that!

COVIELLE: The remarkable fact
is that Turkish can pack
such a wealth of amazing
detail in one phrase.
[HANDING A ROBE TO JOURDAIN] Now,
please slip on this gown
and then kneel yourself down.

CLÉONTE: Cata-mála-lequí
Mama-máma-mouchí!

[JOURDAIN KEEPS HIS HEAD
BOWED. WHEN HE LOOKS UP,
CLÉONTE HAS DISAPPEARED]

JOURDAIN: Was that it? That was quick!

COVIELLE: Indeed! He's quite a slick
operator.

JOURDAIN: He's gone!

COVIELLE: Oh, he's just putting on
some new togs for the nuptials.

[EXIT COVIELLE.
ENTER MADAME JOURDAIN]

MADAME JOURDAIN: Good gracious! What's up
with you this time?
You look a mess.
You're like a fourth rate mime
artiste in fancy dress.
You're an advertisement
for hat-stands,
are you?

JOURDAIN: The impertinence!
How dare you, slattern,
have the cheek
to think that you can speak
like that to me.
I'm a Mamamouchi,
I'll have you know.

MADAME JOURDAIN: That is some sort of
overgrown
potato
I suppose? You great
nitwit!

JOURDAIN: Insect!
You should have more respect
for one as noble
as your husband.

MADAME JOURDAIN: Oh,
baloney!

JOURDAIN: Silence,
or I'll wipe that smile
off you, you snide,
smug-faced, self-satisfied—

MADAME JOURDAIN: Say that outside,
I dare you!

JOURDAIN: I just might.

MADAME JOURDAIN: We'll see who's right.

JOURDAIN: I'd like to see you fight
a Mamamouchi.

MADAME JOURDAIN: I'm not scared of you.

[BLACKOUT]

[LIGHTS. ENTER DORIMÈNE AND DORANTE]

DORIMÈNE: Oh please don't drag
me back in there.
That horrible old hag
might come. It isn't fair.
I won't have her humiliate
me any more.

DORANTE: 'Tis she who will
be feeling sore
this time, I guarantee.
The greatest masquerade
is still to see.

DORIMÈNE: But I'm afraid
that I intend
for once and all to end
this lavish spending
on your part
by pledging myself heart
and soul to you. I know
that is the only
way to stem the flow
of your immoderate
expenditure.

DORANTE: I ask no greater
honour, I am sure.

DORIMÈNE: I do it merely
to stop you from ruining
yourself. We clearly
can't have you
in penury on my
account.

DORANTE: Whilst I
am touched by your concern
I only yearn
to say that all I own
is yours alone
to do with as you choose—

DORIMÈNE: But mark you, who's
this? [ENTER JOURDAIN] It's your friend,
got up in the most trendy
outfit. What a hoot!

DORANTE: Sir, I salute
the great Mamamouchi

and beg to be
allowed to add my voice
to the rejoicing.

JOURDAIN: Heaven shower
you with all the power
of the serpent and
the understanding
of the lion.

DORIMÈNE: Sir,
let me concur
with my friend's sentiments
most heartily.

JOURDAIN: Madame, may your rose-tree
be permanently
free of black-
fly. I'm glad you've come back.
I'm sorry that I let
my wife upset
you as she did.

DORIMÈNE: No matter. I consider
it as evidence
of the intensity
of her regard
for you, the ardour of
her caring love.

JOURDAIN: She is most arduous,
it's true.
My ardour's all for you.

DORANTE: Well, let it not be said
that our friend's new found rank

has turned his head.
We can still bank
on his erstwhile support.

DORIMÈNE: He shows such fortitude
as fits a Paladin.

DORANTE: When shall
we see the Grand Turk's son,
to pay His Wondrous
Highness our respects?

JOURDAIN: He has directed
us to wait while he—
but here he comes!

[ENTER CLÉONTE AND
COVIELLE, STILL DISGUISED]

DORANTE [TO CLÉONTE]: Resplendency,
permit me, your most humble
servant to—

JOURDAIN: The Grand
Turk's son's command
of English is not good.
The only way you can
be understood
is through this man
here. He'll translate
for us. And just you wait
to hear them jabbering
away so incoherently.
It's brilliant!
Listen. [TO COVIELLE] Will
you tell His Grace: my friends

wish to commend
His Excellency's—
er—incontinence.

COVIELLE: Alabala crociam acci borem alabamen.

CLÉONTE: Catalequi tubal ourin soter amalouchen.

COVIELLE: His oriental
Highness was exhorting
heaven that the gentle
rain of fortune
may forever nourish
your seed bed,
that it may flourish
in unlimited
abundance.

[ENTER LUCILE]

JOURDAIN: Daughter dear,
come in and join us. We're
preparing for your wedding.

LUCILE [LAUGHING]: Father, what a dreadful
get-up! You're a card,
our Dad, you really are.

JOURDAIN: Don't sweet-talk me. Now listen.
I've arranged for this incredibly
rich potentate
here to bestow
his hand on yours in marriage.
You'll be on a par
with finest royalty.

LUCILE: Indeed? If you ask me—

JOURDAIN: I didn't. Kindly give
your hand. Must you always
be argumentative?
Do what your father says.

LUCILE: And what if I refuse?

JOURDAIN: Do you want me to lose
my temper?

LUCILE: I don't care.
Would you have me forswear
my true love? I declare
that nothing will deter
me from my solemn oath
whereby I am betrothed
to Cléonte—[SEEING THROUGH
CLEONTE'S DISGUISE] but of course
you have a right to force
me to do as you say
and I must then obey.
[GIVING CLÉONTE HER HAND]
See how I give my hand.
Your wish is my command.

JOURDAIN: Such fine obedience!
I knew she would see sense.

[ENTER MADAME JOURDAIN AND
NICOLE]

MADAME JOURDAIN:
Right! Mind your backs, you lot.
[TO JOURDAIN] What's this, then, idiot?

Next door but one have tipped
me off that you have flipped
your lid at last. They say
Lucile's to wed some play-
acting, mid-eastern bloke.
I take it it's a joke?
Well, answer me, you jerk!

JOURDAIN: The son of the Grand Turk,
no less. You would do well
to show respect. Just tell
this chap here. He'll translate
for you.

MADAME JOURDAIN: Oh no I shan't!
I'll tell your Grand Turk straight
to his face that he can't
expect to barge in here
and go round interfering
with our lives. Lucile
is going to have a real
man for her husband, not
some overblown, tin-pot,
third world aristocrat.

JOURDAIN: Be silent! Stop your prattle.

DORANTE: Should you not be glad
of such an honour, Madam?
Think of the cachet.

MADAME JOURDAIN: And who are you, then, pray,
to offer me advice?

DORIMÈNE: Madame, this is a priceless
honour.

MADAME JOURDAIN: You again!
Did I not make it plain
enough last time. Stop droning
on at me.

DORANTE: We're only
being friendly.

MADAME JOURDAIN: No
thanks!

DORANTE: Wait a minute, though.
Your daughter has agreed
to it.

MADAME JOURDAIN: Has she, indeed?
[TO LUCILE] So Cléonte gets the boot,
does he? How absolutely
loathsome.

JOURDAIN: I say she
shall marry royalty.

MADAME JOURDAIN: And I say you're a twat.

LUCILE: Oh, Mother, please!

MADAME JOURDAIN: You rotten
little egg.

JOURDAIN: Because
my darling daughter does
what I say you chastise
her.

MADAME JOURDAIN: I may exercise
my will as well as you.

COVIELLE: A word, Ma'am, entre nous!

MADAME JOURDAIN: What is it?

COVIELLE: It's a private
word.

MADAME JOURDAIN: No thank you, I've
no wish to hear.

COVIELLE [TO JOURDAIN]: But Sir,
if we can just get her
to listen, she
will certainly
see reason.

JOURDAIN: Let
him speak, then.

MADAME JOURDAIN: Get
lost!

JOURDAIN: Listen!

MADAME JOURDAIN: No!
[COVIELLE DRAGS HER OUT OF
EARSHOT OF THE OTHERS]
Hey you! Let go!

COVIELLE [TO MADAME JOURDAIN]:
Can you not tell
it's me, Covielle?
The Grand Turk's son
is Cléonte, unbeknown
to your
dear husband. Surely

you can see
the point.

[THEY RETURN]

MADAME JOURDAIN: I freely
give consent
for this fine—gent
to wed my daughter.

JOURDAIN: Good! He's brought
her round.

CLÉONTE [FORGETTING HIMSELF]: Hooray!

COVIELLE: His Grace is saying
"May the dove
of peace drop love
from high above
and may your head
be garlanded
with his largess."

JOURDAIN: It's an impressive
language, eh?

MADAME JOURDAIN: No more delay!

COVIELLE: The notary
is due to be
here shortly.

DORANTE: Madam
will be glad,
no doubt, to hear
that she may clear

her mind of fear
for her dear husband's
sake, because
my lady friend
and I intend
to make our vows
of marriage now
as well.

JOURDAIN [ASIDE, TO DORANTE]: Pure genius!
So you mean
you're going to fake
your vows to make
my wife believe
she was deceived
when she suspected
me.

DORANTE [ASIDE, TO JOURDAIN]: Correct!
The best defence
for our pretence,
eh?

JOURDAIN [ASIDE, TO DORANTE]: Yes, indeed!
[CALLING ALOUD] Let us proceed,
then, with the ceremony.
Where's
the notary?
Bring him to me.

MADAME JOURDAIN: What of Nicole?
I see that all
the others are
intent on marrying,

so she
might also?

JOURDAIN: The
interpreter
can marry her. [NICOLE RUSHES INTO COVIELLE'S ARMS]
And as for my
own Missus, I
will give her to
anyone who
will have her.

COVIELLE: Thank you. [ASIDE] Can
there be another man
as foolish or as underwitted
as this one?

[TABLEAU.
BLACKOUT.
THE END]